Buddhist temple life in Laos

Buddhist temple life in Laos

Wat Sok Pa Luang

Photography, text and design by

Ilse and Birgit Schrama

Orchid Press

Ilse and Birgit Schrama
BUDDHIST TEMPLE LIFE IN LAOS: Wat Sok Pa Luang

Orchid Press
P.O. Box 19
Yuttitham Post Office
Bangkok 10907, Thailand
www.orchidbooks.com

Copyright © Orchid Press, 2006. Protected by copyright under the terms of the International Copyright Union: all rights reserved. Except for fair use in book reviews, no part of this publication may be reproduced in any form or by any means, electronic or mechanical, including photocopying, recording, or by any information storage or retrieval system without prior permission in writing from the copyright holder.

ISBN 974-524-073-7

Printed in Thailand

A monk was standing in the doorway with his hands in his pockets and said to us sternly: 'We're guarding the secret of Buddhism here. We can't just let anybody in, you know.' Next to him a group of inquisitive students stood giggling quietly. It was about one o'clock in the afternoon and hundreds of novices had just entered the schoolyard in a great orange cloud of dust.

We had come to the Buddhist school hoping to take some pictures, and attached ourselves to the first English-speaking monk we could find, hoping to be given official permission. We were momentarily thrown by the monk in the doorway's cryptic words. Did he see us as a pair of nosey tourists? Should we expect to be allowed behind these closed doors? It became clear to us that two such curious western women were not an everyday occurrence. Moments later, the tension lifted and the monk turned out to be friendly and helpful. The 'secret' of Buddhism had been a playful comment only to bewilder us.

Introduction

Veiled in the blue exhaust fumes of a chaos of motorbikes, the Buddhist temples spaced along the Mekong River boulevard in Vientiane are havens of peace and quiet. Buddhas in various shapes and sizes, stone, wood, or gold, simple or refined, gaze in silence. From time to time an orange-clad monk idles out of a corner, only to dissolve again in the splendor of the temple. Contemplating the scene for a while, questions arise. What do these people actually do all day? Who are they? What moved them to become monks?

'Wat Sok Pa Luang' bears witness to the day-to-day life of a Buddhist temple in Vientiane, the capital of Laos. We were fascinated by the temple community, and by making this book we aimed to deepen our understanding of the lives of the monks, novices and nuns. The images capture their daily routine; the reflections in the text are their own words. Who better to describe their lives than the monks, novices and nuns themselves? We were struck by their peculiar and sober lives, and tried to imagine ourselves in their place. More and more, we began to realize these splendid temple façades concealed a surprising diversity of souls. Simple and extraordinary people, intelligent and dull, wise and ignorant, self-assured and lowly, successes and personal tragedies; all manner of people treading the path of Buddhism through a multitude of frustrations, longings, ambitions and dreams.

Wat Sok Pa Luang

'Wat' is the word for a temple complex or monastery in Laos. At a wat there are one or more temples and around them are the dwellings of monks, novices and sometimes nuns. Wat Sok Pa Luang, the subject of this book, is situated on the outskirts of Vientiane. In its wooded surroundings there are temples and sleeping quarters, but there is also a sauna and a Buddhist high school. The latter is the only one of its kind in Vientiane and only novices and monks study there. Wat Sok Pa Luang is not the most important, and certainly not the most beautiful wat, though it is the largest in town. Its full name is Wat Mahaphutthawongsa Pa Luang Pa Yai and it was founded around 1915.

About thirty monks, thirty nuns and fifteen novices live at the wat; we never found out exactly how many. We tried to find out in a number of ways, but ended up with about many different answers as there were monks. Wat Sok Pa Luang is one of the few temples in Vientiane where there are also nuns.

In contrast with the monks and novices, the nuns are mostly much older, and indeed most are well over fifty years old. There is one sixteen-year-old nun, but she is the daughter of another nun. In addition a number of temple boys live at Wat Sok Pa Luang, as well as a sweeper, and a few laymen who run the sauna and the little shop. The head of the wat is known as the abbot. It was largely thanks to this highly respected spiritual leader that we were able to make this book.

From the age of twelve, boys can be taken on as novices, and start their apprenticeship. There is a ceremony during which they receive an orange robe, and their heads are shaved. When a novice is twenty, he can join the sangha, the order of monks. If he chooses not to become a monk at this age, then he must leave the community. The life of a monk differs fundamentally from that of a novice. Monks not only have a higher status than novices, they also have to observe much stricter rules and have many more social duties. Novices have only ten precepts and a number of training rules to respect, while the number of rules for monks is 227. In Buddhism the status of nuns is lower than that of monks, and the nuns of Wat Sok Pa Luang are no exception. As nuns are not allowed to undergo full ordination in the Theravada tradition, they are given only eight rules and they live an entirely different kind of life.

The role of the wat in Laotian life

In Laos every suburb and every village has its own temple. The wat is a central point in the neighbourhood, and is integrated with all facets of daily life. The dead are cremated there, some people come to ask advice, and others come to seek help with health problems. Not only are monks present at births and marriages, but also when a new shop is opened, it is customary to ask a monk to bless it. Besides, the temple has the role of disseminating information, for example about illnesses such as Aids. First and foremost it is of course a place where monks, novices and nuns practice Buddhism. But in Laotian temple communities, education is just as important. The majority of children who become novices do so in order to go to school. In many cases the parents are too poor to pay the school fees, or the novices may be orphans, or children with a difficult past. Only a small proportion of the boys come to the wat for purely vocational reasons, and most will in fact leave when they complete their schooling. Temples fulfill an important role in Laotian life: they take care of a range of tasks which are handled by governments and other institutions in most other countries.

The rules

The variant of Buddhism practiced in Laos is Theravada. This movement, to which sixty-five percent of Laotians belong, is also known as southern Buddhism, because it has spread along a route via India, Sri Lanka, Thailand to Myanmar, Cambodia and Laos. Northern Buddhism or Mahayana, is found predominantly in Nepal, Tibet, China, Japan, Korea, Mongolia and Vietnam. Theravada is older than Mahayana and is based on the original texts and teachings of the Buddha.

Theravada places great emphasis on the relief of suffering and the attainment of enlightenment. Suffering, which is present in every person's life, is mainly caused by ignorance. People become too attached to material things, and to their own past and experiences. According to the teachings these things must be relinquished. Mind and body are in a continuous state of flux, and every-thing is impermanent and transitional. Meditation, their most important technique, leads to insight into the nature of the self and to a deeper understanding of the Buddhist doctrine—and, by this means, also to a reduction of suffering.

Buddhist doctrine is put into practice with individual variations, and this is apparent in the way that the rules are observed. At Wat Sok Pa Luang there appear to be very few fixed rules, for example, about how often one must attend morning and evening prayers, when to meditate, how often to take part in the morning alms round, or when to sweep the grounds. We were keen to understand the temple rules, but we became more and more aware that the vinaya was not easy to fathom. The vinaya, an all-encompassing system of rules designed to provide the monks with guidelines for their lives, is intended to facilitate the general order. In some ways it resembles the underlying rules of a political or other social system. To an outsider, it is an impenetrable jungle of rules, and yet those who subscribe to it see it as a part of themselves. We came to realize that these rules were less dogmatic in practice than they at first appeared. Each monk has his own way of living with the rules. What may be acceptable in daily life to one of them may be met with disapproval by another.

Although their daily lives might not harmonize completely with the precepts of pure doctrine, most of the monks have managed to find a good middle course, and this is a result of their long training. In contrast, we noticed that the novices have a much greater struggle with the rules. Like others of their age-group, these youngsters like to run and jump, peek at the girls, listen to music, and they can also be very self-conscious about their pimples. They are curious and candid, funny and often mischievous. For them the rules can be a trial, and in particular the ban on eating after noon. These children burn so much energy that they often end up longing for some food in the evening, and they sometimes secretly eat something. There are several other rules they also have some difficulty with. We remember a conversation with a novice who suddenly remonstrated: do you really think that I get up every morning at four? It was as if he wanted to say: you've seen what life is like here, and it's not always the way you thought it would be, hmm?

The ten precepts are an essential part of the vinaya, and form a central tenet of Buddhist doctrine. These are the prohibitions to kill people and animals, to lie and to steal, the prohibition of sexual contact, and of using drugs or alcohol. As we have described, it is forbidden to eat anything after noon. Amusement, dance and music are not permitted, and the same applies for jewelry and perfumes. Monks are not allowed to sleep in a luxurious bed and it is forbidden for them to possess money. Although some of the rules are open to interpretation, others are absolute, such as the ban on sexual contact. If this rule is broken, a council of monks may be called. If a monk has shown blatant disregard for the rules, he may be told to leave the temple immediately. This is the most serious punishment anyone can receive.

The sangha, or order of monks, tries to keep undesirable behavior inside the walls of the temple, and out of the view of the outside world as much as possible. Members are expected to keep the image of the pure Buddhist intact. They should show a good example, not only to laymen, but also to each other, and this attitude is necessary for the continuation of the order. If they fail to behave according the code of the order, or indeed if they misbehave, they may lose not only the respect of laymen, but also of each other. Bad behavior can jeopardize their existence, because they depend on the donations of others for their food and clothes, and because they depend on each other, as members of all communities do.

Some background

The better we got to know people, the more we became absorbed into the daily life of Wat Sok Pa Luang; gradually the camera ceased to be the centre of attention. Nevertheless, it continued to be a question of testing boundaries and searching for openings. Although we had official permission from the abbot to take pictures, and we were able to move freely, that did not mean that everything could be photographed. Simple things like watching television, and frivolous play sometimes turned out to be against the rules, and could not be photographed for this reason. There were some borderline cases which we decided to show in the book, such as the photos of a novice who is practicing kung fu. It may seem innocent to an outsider, but the fact remains that the novice was breaking the rules.

The delicate balance between what could and could not be photographed had nothing to do with unwillingness or prohibition; we were very hospitably received. The inhabitants of the wat were all extremely warm and helpful, and treated us with respect. Thoughtful, wasting very few words, their considerable reserve called for a careful approach. When telling or explaining something, their lateral way of thinking never ceased to amaze us, and we had to listen with patience. For us, their characteristic manner of weaving around the subject meant it could be easy to lose the thread.

Some subjects were not easily broached. Questions such as: do you want to go on to become a monk, do you want to remain a monk for your whole life, do you ever long for some female company, don't you wish you could have children, nearly always resulted in a shy smile, and not an answer. Once when we asked a nineteen-year-old novice if our curiosity was a bad thing, he said: no, not bad, but strange! That seemed to us to be a very revealing answer. While researching this book we did our best to get hold of documents about the history of Wat Sok Pa Luang and books about Buddhism in Laos. Our library expeditions were ultimately fruitless: each time we arrived full of hope, only to depart empty-handed. The most important university library in Laos, a Buddhist country, had just a single shelf of books about Buddhism. Gradually we realized that the libraries had nothing to offer, and that Laos lacks a developed book culture. The country was isolated from the rest of the world for a long time, and has a small-scale and predominantly agricultural economy. A culture of day-to-day struggle has its effects on the production of books. Clearly, we would have to do without background material, and rely on our own observations. The lack of documents and photographic books about Laotian temple life strengthened our resolve to collect as much material as possible and use it to make a book.

Sometimes it can be impossible to describe a feeling which goes beyond words. Nevertheless, we would like to devote a few sentences to describing the ambience of Wat Sok Pa Luang. For us it was coloured by a vivid palate of sounds. It was a quiet place, and if you heard something it was the rustle of leaves in trees or bushes, barking dogs, cries of children at play, a motorbike of a visiting layman, or the sweeping rhythm of a broom. It was peaceful, and the atmosphere was contemplative. The rumble of the city could be felt, but it kept its distance. When the novices were having fun, it might find expression in a shy smile, but not in unrestrained laughter. If any of them wrestled with emotions such as anger or dissatisfaction, this was apparently resolved internally, and not in the presence of others; a raised voice was something we never heard. Serenity was at its most tangible during the daily services. The chants which winged their way through the shutters of the temple hall, nestled down over the whole terrain. As the cars and scooters outside the gates raced past in all their haste, these chants laid upon the wat a transcendent stillness. Weaving deliberately into the dust and the foliage, these recitations dissolved into the very veins of the trees.

Impermanence

Everything changes. That's the main idea of the Buddha's teachings, and it's something which I have experienced for myself. When I was eleven, my mother died unexpectedly. My father remarried within a year, and shortly after, my stepmother also died. It was then that my father suggested I should become a novice. But I didn't want to do anything, I just missed my mother. Against my will, I became a novice. After living at the wat for a while, I slowly changed. The monks and novices were all kind to me. Some of them became like brothers to me. Nowadays, I don't see my father often, but I have learned to respect him.

ວັດໂສภาบ่าทລอๆ

A novice

This year, I was intending to finish high school. However, I have decided to wait a year to prepare myself for monkhood. At the age of twenty, we are expected to make a choice. Either we have to be ordained as a monk or we choose the secular life. As a novice, I have to live according to ten precepts and seventy-five guidelines, called 'training rules', but a fully ordained monk has at least 227 rules! Becoming a monk means opting for a very particular life style centered around the temple. Not every novice wants that or is capable of it. Some of them want to marry and have children. Should I ever decide to leave the temple, it won't mean turning my back against Buddhism. I will always stay a Buddhist.

Alms round

After sunset, we assemble at the gate for the daily alms round. We walk in three groups through different parts of the neighbourhood. I do this round maybe four times a week. The gifts are important for the temple, and the ritual offerings give the laymen the opportunity to make merit by giving us alms. It's one of the principal ways in which Buddhists can make merit, beside praying and adhering to religious commandments.

An important saying is: Do good and receive good; do evil and you will receive evil.

Fasting

This morning, I helped her with some small tasks. She's the nicest nun at the wat, perhaps as kind as my own mother. While I was rearranging the wood, she prepared some chicken. But at 11 o'clock, there was lunch as well. That was too much; my belly almost exploded! Sometimes I can't control myself, and I'm afraid that I'll be hungry in the afternoon. Slowly I am getting used to not eating after 12 o'clock, but I still find it difficult. Now and then, every novice cheats. In the evening, three days ago, I was very hungry and ate some rice, secretly. But then, I regretted it so much that I couldn't sleep. I said to myself: I would never do this again. But the next evening, my stomach was protesting again. I've noticed that the older monks have less of a problem with this. I understand that fasting is important as a way of learning to control our desires, but for children, I'm inclined to think they should make an exception to the rule!

15

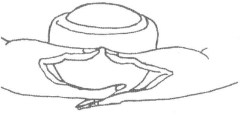

Making merit

Donating food gives laymen the opportunity to gain credit. Together with meditation and adhering to Buddhist teachings, the ritual of making merit helps people in their mental growth. For the novices, on the other side, the alms round is considered as a good exercise, inducing qualities such as humility, unselfishness and compassion.

Yawning

It's very difficult for me to go to bed on time. There are no rules that tell us at what time we have to sleep, but they do expect us to be alert in the morning. Yesterday evening at our house, we talked until it was very late. We have a new novice in the house and I think he was homesick and I wanted to help him settle in. When I finally lay in my bed, it struck me that it was already midnight. This morning, during the chants, I almost fell asleep. Even though the monks sit in front of us, they seem to have eyes in the back of their heads! When I yawned, it was noticed instantly. I admit, some more discipline wouldn't do any harm, but tell me, how do you become a morning person? Is that something you can learn?

19

ເດັກ

My teacher

He is a good teacher and often helps me with Buddhist texts or English. I don't read a lot, because I think it's better to learn from a teacher. Nevertheless, you shouldn't take his words for granted. The Buddha taught us it's important to think for ourselves and to reflect. According to him, that's the only path to wisdom. Will I ever be a wise man? I do hope so! Perhaps it might help if I spent less time on computer games or idling about. Last Sunday, I saw a Bollywood movie with some friends. I suppose these things are a waste of time.

The Buddhist teachings tell us: a good teacher practices what he preaches and preaches what he practices.

Vipassana

Others may not agree with me, but meditation is the best thing I've ever learned. Whenever I have negative feelings, or am angry or sad, I do some meditation. It relaxes my mind and gives me the opportunity to understand my feelings better. Through meditation, negative thoughts can be transformed into positive ones. I sit or lie and observe my breathing and try to look at things as they really are. As technique improves, one can choose other points of concentration. It is a process of self-purification by self-observation. It can be practiced by everyone, at any time, in any place. I do it every day. Once a week I give meditation lessons to people from outside the wat.

Master's degree

In the morning I'm studying at the Lao-American college for a master's degree in English. I've been lucky, since an Australian lady is paying for my studies. Without her, I would never have been able to go beyond high school. My parents only have two small paddy fields. Sometimes, during the monsoon their house gets flushed away by the heavy rainfalls. Initially, my father didn't want me to become a novice. He was a monk himself and knows what it involves. But now he is proud that I'm studying.

Exchange

It is forbidden for us to earn money. I don't have anything against that but it makes life hard for us. We need money for the electricity bills, for schoolbooks, toothpaste, and to take tuk-tuks. Most things cost money and the people who give us food in the morning expect to be paid if we need something from their shop. Sometimes we display religious objects on Saturday at the temple. Laymen come to collect them and give us money in return. We call it the exchange of wares, which is allowed. The laymen get a bargain because the goods are cheaper than when they buy them at the market. We don't make a profit but it gives us a little cash. If you don't have enough money, you feel unhappy.

My duty

My day starts at 3.30 a.m. each morning. I'm one of the principle singers during the morning prayers. Besides that, I have all kinds of other duties. In the morning, I have breakfast with the abbot. After that, I attend any special events that might occur, like a funeral or a birth. I also spend time training the novices. I enjoy that, as I'm rather fond of the little rascals. They are playful and cheerful. Of course, they break the rules sometimes, but most of them are really trying to be a good novice. As long as things don't go too far, I let them go their own way. After all, I was also a child once and I know those pranks will disappear, as they get older. They are at a time of their lives in which they have to develop their conscience. So, I only react if they doggedly refuse to improve their behavior. Then, I look very severe or tell them off and usually that does the trick. It's very clear to them what they may or may not do.

Killing animals

People often think that it is against our principals to eat meat. I don't know why they think so. Does it have something to do with the precept that forbids us to kill men and animals? Probably. We are not allowed to kill animals, but if a layman gives us a piece of chicken, we may eat it as long as the chicken hasn't been killed especially for us. We depend on food that laymen give us and can't just say: we eat this but not that. We eat everything, including snake and fish. Anyway, Lao people don't eat meat every day as it would be too expensive. Someone who eats meat can be pure at heart, while someone who doesn't can be selfish and dishonest. The teaching of the Buddha is about the quality of your heart, not about the contents of your stomach. I love to eat chicken, but my favorite is noodle soup.

Tuk-tuk

The students that come here are from many areas of the city. Usually, to save money, the novices travel together and share the cost of a tuk-tuk. I have it easy, because I live next to the school! This saves me money and gives me the opportunity to take a nap between the lessons. Some of the novices have to walk for more than an hour each day, even when the heat is above 30 degrees. Cycling would be easier, but it's impossible. The monks consider the traffic too dangerous, and besides, walking is better for your health. In the countryside, cycling is quite normal, mainly because the distances are too long for walking.

English

In my early twenties I was a monk, but now I'm an English teacher at the school. I live with my wife and children in a small village, two hours outside of Vientiane. My village is too far to travel daily to be with my family so I also stay overnight during the week in the school building and on the weekends go home. The students are taught subjects such as Lao, Thai, English, mathematics, chemistry, geography and biology. Besides that, we teach them Buddhist subjects. English is a popular subject, but for us it is difficult to satisfy the demand. We can only offer them two hours a week. That is why many students take English lessons at other schools. Most of the novices are aware of why they attend our school: we offer them better prospects. They understand the necessity of a good education and study hard. Naturally, some of them would rather be doing some else, like surfing on the Internet or other distractions.

High school

All the novices in Vientiane attend this Buddhist high school. Although there is currently only one in Vientiane, I've been told that a second one is planned. Rumour has it that the new one will follow Buddhist teachings more strictly. Whatever form it takes, a second school will certainly be welcome. In this school, we have eight hundred students and only three buildings, which is simply not enough. More and more novices come to Vientiane to study all the time. It's government policy to limit class size to no more than 45 students. I really have no idea how we'll ever achieve that. We just can't refuse any students, can we?

ເxະ ເx ແxະ ແx ໂxະ ໂx

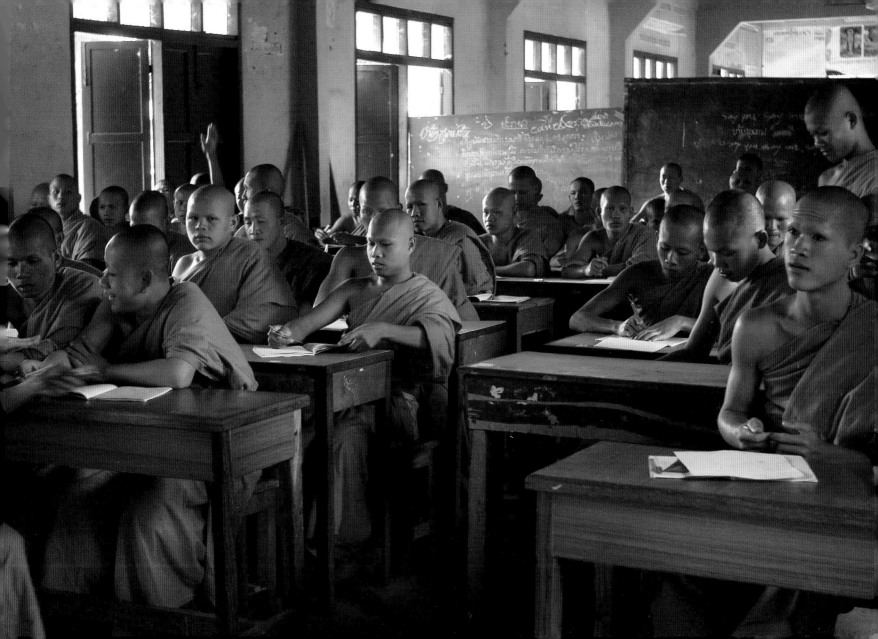

Library

There are ninety pupils in my class. The teacher often complains that we're too noisy, but I think that's inevitable: we have to sit so close to each other you can hardly move. If it's hot and humid outside, it can be quite unbearable in the class. Now I'm on my way to the library. It's only open one afternoon a week, and has books on deep sea diving, soccer, sailing, gardening, airplanes. There's an American lady who collects books and donates them. I've never been in the public library in town because it's too expensive for me.

School fee

If you haven't enough money to pay the school fee, sometimes a monk or a layman will pay it for you. But even if that doesn't happen, there's no need to worry. Several years ago, when I attended the school for the first time, I had no money. My parents didn't have any money and I didn't know anyone else to approach. But no one at the school ever asked me to pay my fee. At public schools, you are refused if you can't pay. As soon as I have finished high school, I will probably disrobe and leave the wat to find a job. With the money earned, I want to follow some courses on electronics, and I also hope to be able to help my parents. They only have a buffalo.

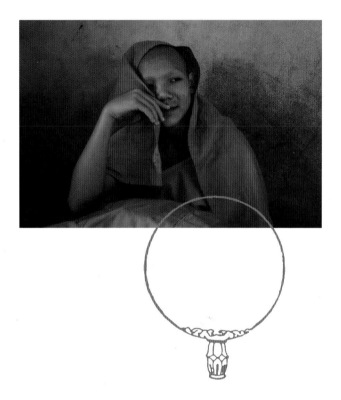

My robe

When I became a novice, I was afraid of my new clothes. I had been used to trousers for thirteen years and friends of mine tried to frightened me, saying you weren't allowed to wear any underwear. The first months, it felt like some kind of ancient costume. Every layman seemed to be watching me when I walked through the streets. Each time I jumped across a puddle, I imagined they were all observing me with disapproval. A monk or a novice ought never to jump. He has to move with grace and tranquility. Now such anxieties and delusions no longer trouble me.

Being naughty

Now and then, we all break a rule. I mean, we are not completely naïve about life outside the gate. If we're bored and looking for some pleasure, we might forget the rules for a moment. Last week, my friend went with a neighbour to the evening market in layman's clothes to drink a banana shake. It might sound innocent, but if a strict monk should find out, he would beat him with a stick, or perhaps even expel him from the wat. Another friend went with his layman friends to a kickboxing match. Afterwards, they all went for a beer. Doing something like that is a thrill, but afterwards the trespassers are usually afraid. They have to be careful. Of course, novices who break the rules all know they are playing with fire, so most of them don't take the risk. Perhaps, they don't feel the need.

Wisdom

Don't ask me what wisdom is; I'm only sixteen! The word wisdom is often used in the teachings of Buddhism and I know that obtaining wisdom is one of the most important aims in life. But how does one become a wise man? Because I have heard them so often, many views are known to me. For example: it is not about knowledge of facts, but about insight, honesty and truth. Or that we have to try to love our enemies. I'm afraid it would take me at least a thousand years to become a man of wisdom! But now, let's talk about something else. It's tiring to talk about such complicated matters! There is no magic formula for wisdom. Either you are a wise man or you become one.

Palm leaves

Since time immemorial, Buddhist texts have been inscribed on palm leaves. Using a sharp needle, the letters are scratched onto the surface. The words become visible through treatment of the grooves with a coloured resin. Nowadays, scriptures are printed, which is much cheaper. The language used is either Pali or Sanskrit, ancient tongues only used in a sacred context. We use these scriptures during ceremonies. The writings can cover almost any subject: this one, for example, is about selfishness. The words are slightly cryptic, but we read that a selfish man is unable to put himself in the position of someone else. We have to battle the selfishness by purification of the mind so that compassion can take its place. Still, the scriptures are less important than learning from our own experience. Buddhists agree that it is foolish to mistake the written word for the reality toward which it points: scriptures possess no value in themselves.

Layer by layer

At the moment, the temperature is pleasant, but in the time of the monsoon, it rises to thirty degrees or more and it becomes very humid. Sometimes, that can be too much for me. Not without some envy, I look at the laymen in their loose clothes. My robe may look simple, but don't be fooled. With a single robe, you can cover two beds, perhaps even three! If my friends are waiting for me, and I don't take the time to wrap every layer carefully, I can get into a real muddle. At the wat, I prefer to wear a cotton shirt: it's less complicated and doesn't restrict movement. That way I hope my robe will keep it's colour longer too!

Full moon

Shaving takes place once a month, on the day before full moon. That's today, and I've just been. Before afternoon prayers, we're all expected to shave. If you don't make the effort you'll certainly be noticed among all those shiny heads.

Now I'm off to fetch my cap; I'm cold! You might think I'm a bit of a wimp, wearing a cap in this kind of temperature. But I can't help it: to me it's rather chilly!

Calendar

Full moon is an important day for us. More people than normal come to the wat to make offerings, and you must have a good reason for not being at the prayers. But also new moon, first quarter and last quarter are special, and these are called Buddhist days. The most beautiful ceremony of the year is when we celebrate the birth, enlightenment and death of the Buddha. That's something I look forward to. Otherwise, we don't have many festivals at our wat.

Sticky rice

We eat plenty of rice, mostly sticky rice. If there's any left, the temple boys sometimes make rice cookies, or it is given to the chickens. We also get fruit bars, biscuits, vegetables and sometimes a little money. First, the monks eat their fill, then the novices are next, and if the temple boys are out of luck, there may only be rice left. We are supposed to share the food fairly, but sometimes when a monk has a bad temper, or wants to 'discipline' a novice, he might keep some food for himself. Meals are never taken for granted. That's not only because we fast after our midday meal, but also because we never know what food there will be the following day. Not that we're ever likely to go hungry for long: we're no paupers. There are plenty of families who, like us, eat twice a day simply because they don't have enough for three meals. They manage to get used to this.

University

Earlier, when I was just a very small boy, I liked to go to the chants in the village temple.

Now I have left the village to go the high school in Vientiane. Sometimes, I do miss playing

with my friends in the river. When I visit my family, I sometime go swimming with the others.

They keep it secret because they know that I'm not allowed to swim. In a few years, when I

have passed my exams, I would like to go to a Buddhist university abroad, for example in

Bangkok. There are only a few Buddhist universities in the world. We'll see; if you don't

have the money, you have to be lucky to be chosen.

Toothbrush

The wat has to look clean because of the coming festival. Today, the abbot has inspected all the temples. I was just walking around when he beckoned towards me and put me to work. I was planning to do some study, but it will have to wait. We have to scrub the statues with a toothbrush and a small piece of cloth. Ledge by ledge! There isn't another novice in sight. I think the others have locked themselves in their rooms.

Brrrr...

Today, it's really very cold and this isn't normal for the time of the year! We are going to stay in bed all day. The novices like to come here. The monk who lives in this house is a friendly, good-tempered man. The only thing that he can't stand is when the novices are being too noisy. Sometimes, they peek at the girls who are living in the university campus next to us. They find this very amusing. The elder monk pretends that he doesn't see or hear it. Lately, he repaired an old television for them so that they could watch kickboxing. He fixes everything that is broken. He studied electronics, but he will never do something just for himself. If he can make others happy then that is enough for him to be happy.

My master

In about six months I'll be leaving for the temple of my master Phra Ajahn Xali Khantasali. He used to be abbot here at Wat Sok Pa Luang. I'm now living in his former house. Two years ago, he went to the woods where he spent his time meditating. When he came back to Vientiane, he set up his own temple. I have a great respect for him and want to help him with my English. Probably, many foreigners will come to visit his place; there are over four thousand monks who regard him as their master. They started building the temple a few months ago; it will become the biggest one in Vientiane. There will also be a Buddhist high school where they will teach Buddhist learning exclusively. The school will be more puritan than our own school, and meant for novices who really want to become monks.

After sunset

He's very good at kung fu. All the novices want to have him as a teacher. We're not allowed to practice kung fu, but it's tolerated, as long as it doesn't draw too much attention. We practice in the bushes, mostly after sunset. Sports are forbidden, unfortunately. In early times, the monks walked from village to village, the whole day long. They had plenty of exercise. But our lives are different; we spend so much time sitting in the school seats. Kung fu is one of the most popular sports in Laos. Everybody watches it on television; we also, but behind closed doors!

Temple boy

Two years ago, I decided to become a temple boy. I wanted more freedom after being a novice for so long. Most houses at the wat have a temple boy. He cooks, washes, cleans the house and trims the trees. I also teach one of the monks English. The wat has been my salvation. At the age of eight, my parents died. They were working in the forest when one of the landmines exploded. They were instantly killed. I'll never forget the image of parts of their bodies, littered on the ground. Still, I often dream about it. After this tragedy, I decided to become a novice. My brothers and grandmother are still living in the village, but life is hard. They feed themselves from what they can find in the jungle and they have a small piece of rice land. I have received a scholarship for the Lao-American College. It's the best school in Laos. I've been lucky.

Kung fu

It was wrong of me to let you witness this kung fu exercise. We had fun, I got a bit carried away with the others. I shouldn't have done it. I regret it. It's not good if people see these pictures. We have to make a good example.

According to the Buddhist teachings a mistake isn't criminal or bad, as long as a novice realizes that he was wrong. This realization is much more important than the mistake itself.

Our houses

All the houses are occupied, so I am living in this small temple. Everyone can look inside, but that's no problem. Sometimes, ten novices are sitting here watching television. It doesn't matter to me where I'm living. Everyone has his own wishes and style: one puts up posters, another one likes to place small candles. Some of the nuns don't mind at all and are living in empty rooms. Often, they don't even have a mattress; they just sleep on a mat. The nun who is living at the gate has a big house with two floors, but it is completely empty except for a small mat and a cushion. Two novices are living in the hall of prayer and they have made their own house out of two wardrobes.

Time

If I need to know the time, I look at the sun and at important moments there is always the bell of the school or the gong in the temple hall. The roll of drums that you can hear at four o'clock at night through the whole town, is meant for the early risers. I prefer to wake up with the crowing of the roosters. None of us have watches as it's forbidden to wear any jewelry. I also don't have a diary but take each day as it comes. Others are committed to time schedules, but really, for us, the fewer disturbances, the better. Yesterday I wanted to go to the afternoon service, but on my way I bumped into a good friend who had lived here for a long time. I didn't recognize him at first because his hair was so long. We had a good talk. He told me about his new girl friend, and he was radiant with happiness.

Donation

Because it's my responsibility, I generally take care of these kinds of painting jobs. We hired the painters, because the novices and monks have other things to do. The big temple can be painted because our abbot has received a donation from a monk. Next month, there will be a festival, so by then, the temples should look very shiny. There will be some special visitors from Thailand. Yesterday, we explained to the novices how to welcome our Thai friends in the friendliest way. The painting of the outer walls is nearly ready. Tomorrow we will start with the inside of the temples. The Buddha statues will also be cleaned. They just raised the scaffolding for this. This temple is only used for the most important occasions. The daily chants are performed in the hall as it's less dark and therefore gives a feeling of openness.

My family

In the village were I was born, I attended the temple school but the education was rather poor. That's why I came to Vientiane. I miss my family and don't get to see them very often. This week, I planned to visit them because it had been a while since I heard anything from them. But this morning my mother called and told me everything's fine. Now I'll postpone the trip, and maybe go there in a few months' time.

Malaria

In the morning, I ring the bell in the temple hall. It's my responsibility and therefore I have to get up at 3.30 a.m. I'm living in the hall together with another novice. Sometimes I feel lonely. I have no family left. My parents died five years ago; my father at the age of 40 years from malaria, several months later my mother as a result of an unknown disease. She was ill; she suddenly died. After their deaths, I became a novice, which was the only possibility. I have a brother, but I never see him and the last thing I heard was that he was married. Although the wat has given me the opportunity to make something out of my life, I am still afraid of the future. I have to do everything for myself. Today, I missed breakfast because I wanted to study Japanese. I'm also afraid of mosquitoes. At present, there are no mosquitoes but they will surely return in the rain season. I would like to go to bed because I'm so tired.

Crazy old monk

The novices often make fun of him. They secretly take some food from his house and throw little stones on his roof. Or they drop some water over him when is lying asleep. Well, he asks for it. He doesn't share things with others. Often, bags of fruit are rotting in his house. He begs for money despite having plenty of it himself and he abuses his position. Once he sent the temple boy in the middle of the night to buy eggs - as if you can buy them in the middle of the night! He's selfish and that's against the teachings of the Buddha. His life story up until now also doesn't do him justice. At the age of fifty, he fell in love with a girl of twenty-one years. They got married and had a child. But three years ago, he returned to the wat. I don't know why. He's 86 now. I don't know if he is divorced from his wife but they are still in contact with each other. Daily, his son brings him food, but he never stays longer than five minutes. In the past, the old monk was highly respected but those days are gone. I'm afraid that something has gone wrong in his head. In the morning, he calls out: 'bonjour!' Maybe in his mind he is still living in the time when he studied at a French university.

จอก

Locals

The laymen like to be here. They help
to sweep the floors and pick up odd
jobs here and there. Some of them are
coming to see the abbot or a monk to
make merit. During festivals, like last
week, there are always many laymen.
They came to listen to the dharma
reflections. There was also a classical
Lao dance and music performance
that was very impressive. People had
brought all kind of things, like milk,
chocolate, fruit, clothes, money and
even beer. As a temple boy, I'm
allowed to drink beer. I got some
drinks, because I worked so hard in
preparation for the festival, placing
the chairs, preparing the sleeping
places and the food. Normally, I
never drink beer; that's why I was
a little drunk.

Karma

Karma has to do with cause and consequence. If I treat you badly, you probably will treat me badly also. If I kill a bird with a stone then I disturb the natural state of things. We must be aware that our actions have a consequence in the future. If you radiate happiness, you will also recall this. I'm explaining it a little too simply; it is much more complicated than this…

Our sweeper

He sweeps the whole day long. The leaves fall from the trees, month after month. At twilight, he burns the leaves that he swept during the day. It's nice and warm and prevents the mosquitoes from coming. Often, we gather around the fire. Our sweeper is a nice man; he will never leave the wat. How old he is? He can't remember anymore. I think that he is in his seventies. He served in the army in the north of Laos. When he came back to Vientiane, it turned out that his family had emigrated to America. Since then, he has been living here for over ten years. He always looks happy, that is because of the sweeping. He doesn't need dharma lessons. He would be a good monk, but that's not a question; he is who he is.

High tech

Even though they don't have the money for it, the novices want to have music, a television, and a computer. We have only a few televisions and telephones at the wat; some novices have a mobile phone. I had one, but I have put it away. They all came to borrow my phone and after two weeks, my phone card was finished. The Internet is also very popular and is causing a stir. Personally, I find the Internet very practical for email. But monks who have their own website are going a step too far for me. About half of the monks who are living here, think we should keep up with modern times; the other half don't want to change. I don't know which side I'm on.

Video clips

He has a DVD-player, a camcorder and almost a hundred video clips. Regularly, his friends come to watch television. His brother and sister are living in America and sometimes send him some money. It would be better if he shared the money, but no-one can force him. As a result, unkind remarks are made about him. Perhaps the others are jealous. I don't know. In any case, the comments don't seem to have any effect on him. He has his own little house. I think that more members of his family are monks. During meetings, he sometime takes the place of the abbot. Speaking for myself, I do like him although he is a little strange. Last year, he adopted a boy from a poor family. His family is now raising the baby. When the boy becomes the age of six, the wat will become his new house. I don't fully understand, but I like it anyway. There are so many children with no future.

Paddy fields

Like most of the novices, I hardly go anywhere. It distracts me. I find it hard to deal with all the impressions. Nevertheless, I like to walk along the rice lands. It reminds me of the village where I was born. I imagine my mother working on her own field. It gives me a peaceful and quiet feeling, even though I know that living in the countryside is hard. In about two months, I will go to visit my mother because there will be a festival. At first, I planned to go with a monk who is from the same village, but last week he disrobed and left the wat. He has gone north to find a job. I have known for a while that he would leave us at a certain moment. It wasn't his real mission in life to be a monk. I'll miss him, because he is a true friend.

Possession

I like books and magazines and often go to the market to read them. I especially enjoy Thai magazines which are written for women! I don't have the money to buy them. I have only a few books: A photo book on Laos, a history book, a comic magazine about the life of the Buddha, a book about fortune telling and some magazines on Buddhism. I like to read, but I also like to travel. But, it isn't proper to have things or want to travel. According to the teachings, we may only possess some clothes, a belt, an umbrella, a begging bowl, a bed and a razor knife. Although most of us have more than that, the rules are meant to teach us to live without luxuries.

Buddha Park

Yesterday, I went on a great journey! Well, not to some far country, but I have been close to the Thai border. We passed the Friendship Bridge. It's only a few years old and paid for by the Australian government. There was no one else on the bridge, beside some big trucks on their way to China or Thailand. After the Friendship Bridge, we went to the Buddha Park. I had never been there before. I seldom leave the wat, only if I have to go to school. The Buddha Park was half an hour drive. I like all the Buddha statues, but I find the one where the Buddha is lying down the most beautiful. It's also the biggest. The Buddha was nearly eighty years old and about to die.

Nuns

The Buddha didn't forbid us to enter the sangha, but he also didn't encourage us. Nowadays, more and more nuns are coming to live at the wat. We have our own personal missions within society. During the day, we visit people or work on special projects. Recently, I informed laywomen about the risks of Aids. It was during a large Aids campaign. Almost one third of the women present had never heard of Aids. For us nuns, it's easier to talk to them about such delicate matters than it is for the monks. We are not allowed to walk on the dawn alms round in the morning like the monks and novices. The laymen come to us with food or we buy it ourselves or trade something else for food. I knit caps and vests. In exchange, the monks give me food or money.

Walk meditation

What is walk meditation? How does it work? You stand in a relaxed manner, shut your eyes and feel that your feet are making contact with the earth. Slowly, you rise your foot and place it just in front of your other foot. You are aware of every move you make. You walk using the rhythm of your respiration, going slowly or faster, your concentration remains with your feet, your movements and your breathing. What counts is the level of concentration that you achieve. You can walk in a circle or just in a straight line, whichever doesn't matter. In fact, you can meditate wherever you want, even if you are waiting on a bus. The sole aim of meditation is to become aware of the here and the now.

Young and old

Before I became a nun, I was married. We had a son and a daughter. My son was a novice, but unfortunately, he disrobed and left the wat. Now I'm living here together with my sixteen-year-old daughter. I presume that the nuns are more pure than the monks, which is understandable. Most of us are old and have a life behind us. The novices and monks are young; they are standing at the beginning and look towards their future with hope. I think, at our age, the words of the Buddha have a greater impact. We have less trouble with anger, greed and suffering. The nun who lives next door has taken her grandson in. She is very old, but has to take care of him. His parents died last year. He has become a temple boy, which allows him to live here. The boy is still going to a public school in the neighbourhood, but he will proba-bly become a novice at the age of twelve.

My stepmother

Everyone is very fond of her. Just like the rest, I also visit her daily, for a small chat or to help her with some work. This week is quiet, because she has gone to a special week of meditation. She has been a nun for over twenty-eight years now. When she was nineteen, she entered as a nun. We have no idea why she decided to become a nun. Somewhere, there is a secret in her past. I have often asked her for her reasons, but she never talks about them. I call her my step-mother, but we give every woman who's good to us that title. I have to say, if I didn't have a mother, I would be very glad if she would be mine!

Sauna

Actually, the sauna is my sister's, but
she doesn't have the time for it. She is
meditating all day long. That's why she
asked me to take care of the sauna.
Most of the visitors are from outside
and are both men and women. The
herbal steam bath has a curing effect,
especially if you let the herbs act upon
your skin for a while. On the veranda,
I serve herbal tea. There are always a
few masseurs present. If they have no
clients, they massage each other. We
need twenty visitors daily to cover the
costs. In the evening, the sauna is open
for novices and monks. For them, it is
free. But the novices don't come so
often, they like to peep at the visitors
while sitting in the bushes.

111

Wat paa

Once Wat Sok Pa Luang was a 'wat paa', a forest temple. The wat was situated in a forest outside the city and at that time, it was much larger. Many foreign monks came to visit the wat because it was a very quiet and peaceful place. Hardly any laymen were living in its surroundings. In the last decade, the wat has become more and more a local temple. Vientiane has grown very fast, and as a result the wat is now located in the centre of one of it's districts. The municipality has repeatedly bought land. I have heard that they are trying to buy another piece to build a hotel. Probably, that won't happen, but the taking away of local land continues. The neighbourhood is very popular. It's not only the municipality; also rich people are buying land. Look around, they all built their own little palaces, they buy what they want to have.

The wat shop

The little shop at the wat, just besides the entrance, is being kept by a Lao family. They sell fruit juice, toothpaste, toothbrushes, soap powder, tea, milk, noodle soup, coca-cola, sweets and so on. Sometime, there are hawkers at the wat. They sell other things like scissors, pencils, exercise books, batteries and combs. Actually, I don't know why the little shop is at the wat. They would do more business outside the gate. Perhaps they like it over here. Anyway, they are good Buddhists and keep themselves to the five precepts that laymen are supposed to act within. The precepts are: not killing, not stealing, not lying, not being involved in sexual misconduct and the last one, abstaining from alcohol and drugs.

Reading

When I was a young girl, I had to work on the rice lands. Only my older brothers were allowed to go to school. My parents didn't have money for my school fee. In the countryside, many girls still don't attend school. Like me, they can't read or write. The government is trying to change the situation, but progress is slow. There's a lack of teachers, and the children's labour is badly needed on the land. The parents keep the girls at home at first, like me. Now, I am too old to learn how to read and write. But, happily, there's a woman living in the neighbourhood who regularly reads to us.

Silence

As fewer foreign monks came to visit the wat, the sauna fell into decay. I thought that was a pity. That's why I rebuilt it completely, painted the wood, planted a new herbal garden and placed some new trails. For over ten years, I have been running the sauna. Now, it's going well and the time has come for me to stop. Soon, I will be leaving for another wat. I'm becoming old and it's getting more and more noisy here. The whole day long, students from the high school are walking in and out, the novices are playing music and the traffic is increasing. I like the silence and want to concentrate entirely on meditation. My sister and some other members of the family will take over the control of the sauna. But occasionally, I will visit the herbal garden and see how it's going. Herbs are not weeds. Weeds don't need special care. Besides, I want to pass on my knowledge to my niece. Otherwise, it will become lost.

119

The abbot

Phra Ajahn Bramma Visanandho is the abbot or the head of the wat. According to the standards of Laos and other nearby countries our wat is well organized. The temples and the grounds look well cared for, the novices, monks and nuns are known for their hospitality, and there are no unpleasant infectious diseases. During the day, the abbot receives laymen from the neighbourhood, but also people from other places. Usually, they come to him to ask his advice or they come to make merit. Sometimes, when they have problems with their health, he is able to help them with his healing knowledge. The practical side of managing the wat lies in the hands of a few monks. They know exactly what is going on. Still, there isn't much that escapes the abbot. If there is something going on which is important, he is one of the first to know. In the morning, he has breakfast with some monks and then they go through all kinds of matters. He's a highly respected man with a gentle character. Dedicated and wise.

Wat Sok Pa Luang

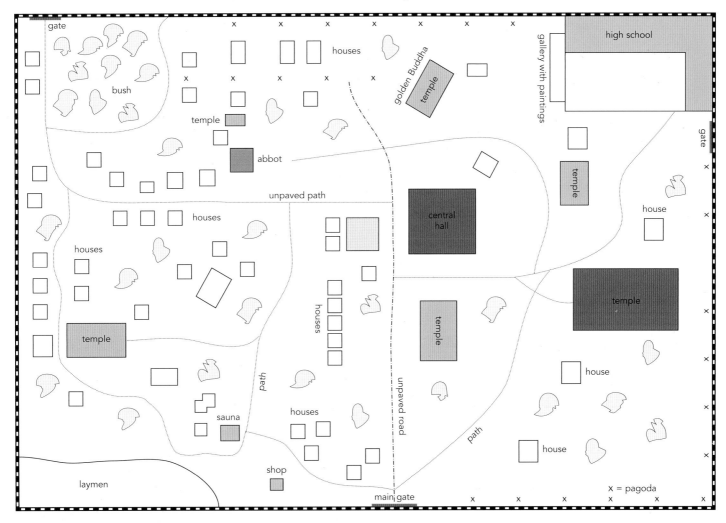

gate

houses

bush

golden Buddha

temple

high school

gallery with paintings

gate

temple

abbot

unpaved path

house

houses

central hall

temple

houses

house

houses

temple

path

temple

house

sauna

houses

unpaved road

path

house

laymen

shop

main gate

x = pagoda

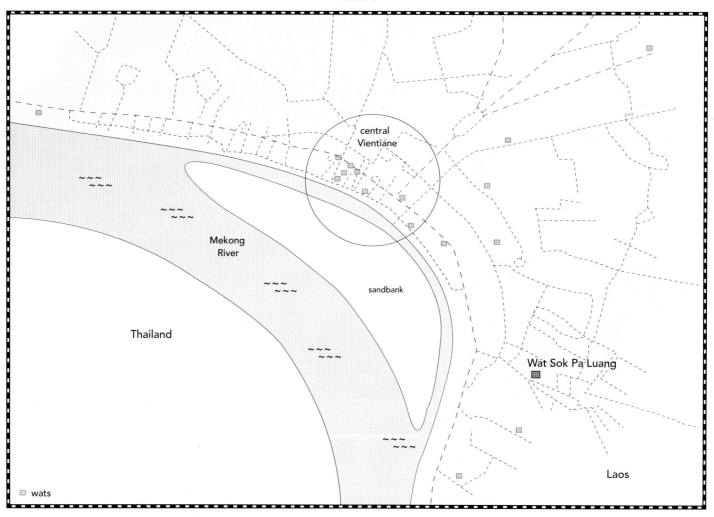

central
Vientiane

Mekong
River

sandbank

Thailand

Wat Sok Pa Luang

Laos

wats

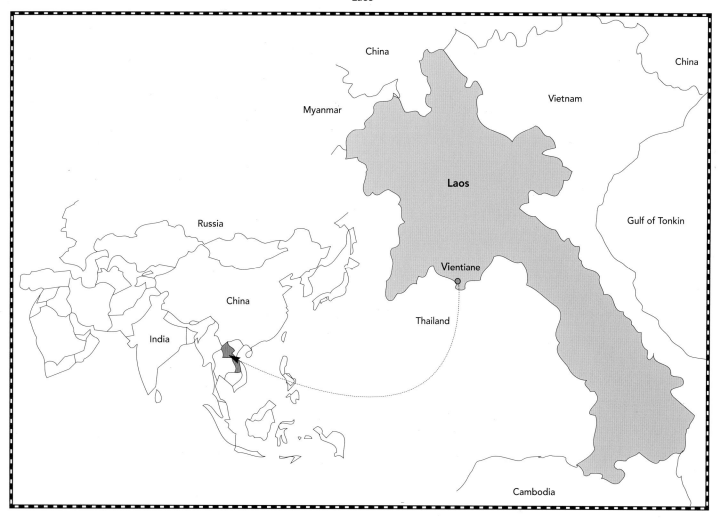

China

China

Myanmar

Vietnam

Laos

Gulf of Tonkin

Russia

China

Vientiane

India

Thailand

Cambodia

Acknowledgements

We would like to thank the following people for their generous assistance:

Phra Ajahn Bramma Visanandho, the abbot of Wat Sok Pa Luang;

Ministry of Education of the Lao P.D.R.;

Office of Lao Buddhist Fellowship Organization in Vientiane;

Buddhist Upper Secondary School, the director and teachers;

The monks, novices, nuns, temple boys and the sweeper of Wat Sok Pa Luang - for their open, helpful ways and willingness to share their lives with us;

Phet Panthavong, Kuan, Faeng and novice Sivilay for the translations made during our stay;

Magnus Robb, Bram de Klerck and Anna McMichael for the translations of the text.

Privacy

In order to protect the privacy of some of the more candid monks and novices, some of the texts do not refer directly to the photos to which they are adjacent. It was not always clear to them or to us what the consequences of their words or actions might be. We do not intend to embarrass or bring discredit to any of the monks or novices, and to this end the dissociation of text and image seemed to be a good choice.

Graphic images

The graphic images used in the book are from Laos. Besides Buddhist symbols, these are decorative temple motifs and images from school books. On page 9 the name Wat Sok Pa Luang is written in Lao.

Colophon

Concept, photography, text and design by Ilse and Birgit Schrama

www.dezusjesschrama.nl